1

Readers who are interested in contacting the
author with queries or business opportunities are invited to
email thepinkerprint@gmail.com
This edition self-published via www.blurb.com in 2016 by the
author Chimson Lawson-Jack
ISBN 978 1530156252

The Pinker Print

Intro

The rocky road to self-love (and indeed self-publishing) is a long and painful journey not made any easier by having an uncompromising stubbornness to not remove my heels whilst trotting along the cobbled streets. Luckily for me, my path is well lit and of solid foundations. God has provided me with all the tools I need to survive and that includes, The Pinker Print...

Think Pink

Amongst my various friendship groups, I would hope to be seen as the "joker". I could also, if given the time, moonlight as the "hippy". I love to give motivational speeches and spells of encouragement to anyone willing to open an ear long enough. With wistful "save the world" graces, I tell brilliant, long winded stories full of painfully witty metaphors and an alarming amount of make-believe adjectives. I crack jokes, re-tell tales to gruesome kids and I chase happiness with a technicolour dream catcher.
But like a dog idiotically after its own tail, I just cannot grasp it.

Because I am suffocating.

So far drowned beneath the safety net of my control. So deprived of light that when I look down the tunnel, I pray for any oncoming traffic. So trapped in the realms of my thoughts, that even the idea of freedom can no longer offer sweet, nor sour solace. The acidic terror of admitting such an outlandish mental confusion even to myself, is enough to wire shut the nervous gate between my psyche and tongue. The fear of whispering my crazy into existence far stronger than any desire to cure it.

But it's okay.

It's okay because I am not alone in my feelings of involuntary incarceration.

As wayward as my thoughts and fluctuating hormonal emotions may be, never once have I deliberated the need for therapy or any mood-numbing pill. Women were built for this shit. Designed for diversity.

Women are not compiled of glitter, rubies and pink sugar frosting. We bruise, we bleed, we fall down seven and stand up eight, we live through the greys and cry to the skies, WE are fuelled by an unearthly power from God and the buried sanctuary from each other.

The matters of my own heart are fragile and incomplete but my strength comes from knowing that no matter how alien each strung up sentence from my mind sounds to me, it will ring true as a regular normality to some woman, somewhere. Women are here to create the pathway of womanhood and tightly clasp our anticipation drenched palms to lead and guide us down it. If the yellow brick road already exists then of course finding the Wizard becomes a little more possible.

I am a girl's girl. I think pink and still believe in a resurrected sisterhood. Women inspire me. The whole appearance and character of a woman can render me fascinated for minutes, hours. The courageous women long before me have sparked fires and revolutions. The women in my present accompany me through the timely tribulations on this journey of figuring shit out.

But it's the women of my future that captivate me with the most prioritised force.

I may be the woman of my own future but somewhere out there, in the reverie of destiny, there are women who have already passed this life exam with flying colours. Women who can offer a digital embrace and ensure me that this time will pass and knowingly blame a cocktail of various hormones for why I feel certain ways.

Amenity.

When it came to writing The Pinker Print, I had no doubt in my mind for who my target audience would be. I alone cannot restore the trust in females to see their fellow gender as more than back stabbing, man stealing hussies, but I can provide a voice, a home, my own digital embrace for the girls growing up as lost as I am but without the reassurance that we are all on the same rocky road.

Growing up is equal parts difficult, surprising, exciting and frightening. Just when you think you have levelled up, you have to face the big fat boss with two heads and a briefcase full of grenades. The journey to adulthood is rough, but at least we can all take joy in the fact that we do not walk alone. Take joy and find peace in the fact that I am going through the shits with you.

Believe in pink.

The

Feminist

"Well behaved women seldom make history."
Laurel Thatcher Ulrich

"You're not a typical feminist though, you're different". Ah so there it is, one of those compliments engulfed in flame throwing insult. As I feel his acidic words burn through the outer layer of my now raging skin, I find a way to bite my tongue and patiently ask, "How" then adding a LOL with too many o's to effectively mask my painful discomfort – this Decepticon worthy act is probably part of the reason I am not a "typical feminist".

My poor, unexpected sexist then went on to say that the reason I cannot be classified as a regular feminist was because I like men, not just sexually but generally. He's right, I do like men, why wouldn't I? I like my brother, my uncles and my cousins. I like my friends, my bosses and my doctor. I do indeed "like" men but at this moment in time, I certainly do not like *him*.

What an earth has being a feminist got to do with liking people? And don't even get me started on the fact that I actually decide whether or not to give someone my attention based on the content of their character and not their undergarments – I like as many men as I do women, I don't discriminate because that's kind of the whole fucking point of feminism you idiot…

…Is what I should have said, but instead, I laughed some more, this time capitalising the L's and O's. "Well duhhh, that's kind of the whole point" I said, encasing my over-achieving attempt at non-threatening politeness with several cheerful looking emojis.

What the hell was I doing? And more importantly, what on earth was so funny? My fingers may have been laughing their asses off but in reality, my ass and its hole were very firmly clenched. I have no idea why, but to this completely detachable stranger, I wanted to be perceived as a nonchalant, love-for-all, happy-go-lucky-and-slightly-flirty feminist instead of just being seen for the I-don't-really-give-a-shit, lazy, human being I am. I may not have come across as a "typical feminist" but I was definitely excreting vibes of a typical dickhead.

As a woman, I can easily admit when I've been a bit of a dickhead, it's one of my many benevolent talents and unfortunately, I've had to send many an apologetic text message in my time. If I could send one to myself at this precise moment, it would probably look a little something like this:

"Sigh. Before you say anything, I already know what I've done and yes I am sorry. I'm sorry I played with the saturation dial on your hyper-hued personality to try and get you to be a closer colour match to the shade of femininity. I'm sorry I resurrected your own archaic thoughts of a "likeable woman" and played them out to and through you whilst you suffered over a very trivial conversation with a very insignificant imbecile of a "man". I'm sorry I made you look like a dickhead…again but on the plus side, he probably wants to sleep with you now! Lol jk, nobody fancies the feminist. Sorry for the essay, please reply x"

And indeed nobody does fancy the feminist – not a typical one anyway and I'm sure that was his whole point of the soul snatching complinsult (compliment+insult). Guys don't want an over opinionated, underwaxed, non-conforming, non-bra wearing, loud, butch, angry thing for a girlfriend. Typical guys do not want typical feminists. Typical guys do not want girls who care that British women earn just 78 percent of a man's wage in 2015, or those who refuse to stay silent about the #everydaysexism they encounter, or women who think it's utterly mortifying that a young woman going out at night has to take certain precautions to avoid being raped on her way home – you know, simple things like not looking too sexy or whatever. A typical lad does not want a lady who thinks more time should be spent educating and rehabilitating men away from society's cathartic rape culture. A typical man wants to marry a smiling, cooking, birthing, machine who also works. A cute, independent woman who's not so secretly dependent on him. A typical man does not want a typical feminist, but a 1950s stereotypical woman.

I could now take this essay into a different direction discussing the way the patriarchy has fetishized the roles of the "good" and "bad" woman. We have all heard the lyrics, the memes, the quotes and the speeches, for a woman to be truly desirable she must be "a lady in the streets but a freak in the sheets". To the outside world she is quiet, clever and innocuous. She is silently aloof to all the wrong doings and injustices to fellow women and humans and unsympathetic to the plight of those outside her social sphere because she is more concerned with crossing her legs on the tube. But at home, my goodness at home she becomes herself, her true self, her slut self. The lady must become the seductress, sucking and fucking without causing a raucous. She now oozes sex appeal and security, her confidence overflowing and intertwining with the pre-cum being secreted from a man just on the thought of this fantasy. A typical man wants a good girl who moonlights as bad. A typical man wants a non-feminist, fully compliant babe who transforms into a rebellious, bad bitch in bed. Now I know I've called the decepticon card already, but all this acting sounds like a fucking headache.

It really doesn't matter what the typical feminist is, or was I should say and to be honest, the defective traits of the typical man are also irrelevant. We are all of an age where we know better now. We are the generation of acceptance and individualism. We have the elasticity to welcome other cultures, beliefs and mismatched genitalia – it's about time we welcome different types of feminists, after all I quite like wearing bras.

Disclaimer: Yes I have spent the last 1000 words making rather invalid generalisations, but the patriarchy did it first, and as you know, I'm all about equality.

Love

Oh, to be loved.

Speaking from the heart, my heart, I can assure you that there is no better feeling than reciprocated love. There is no emotion that evokes such a spectrum of high octaned feeling as *this* L word yet so many young women are ruefully exchanging love for a lesser, cheaper, imitating feeling on the black market of Love.

The other L word. Lust. The naughty, intoxicating L word with a stronger, hotter magnetic pull. On first instance, the confusion is defendable, lust feels like love, its power and heat portraying the equator when in fact, it is only the ray of sunshine on this Earth, not the belt around it. Temporary and always followed by darkness.

Lust is the over imagined King of the night who gallops into our heads, leaving horse manure at the door, then boorishly, yet still unbeknownst to the pawn, sets off with every last bit of common sense once had. Check mate indeed.

But love steals from us too. Love seductively erodes common sense from even the smartest, pretty perfect of girls and although this is done at an obscurely slower pace than its impulsively callow cousin, we are still left with more than a few spotlights out after its home visit.

From an uncomfortably young age, women are taught to be the weaker, dumber, less valued counterpart in what is meant to be an emotional level playing field. Against our will, we are regulated and regimented to grow up, stupid, crazy and dangerously in love.

In fairy tales, we are taught to be too patient, too forgiving, distressed damsels who have to kiss amphibians, dance with beasts and lose rather important parts of our outfits to fall in love. We are taught we must lose to gain. We are taught that even though we had obsessively coveted this season's, intricately crafted glass slipper, we must now give that up, to win over a sock-less twat in penny loafers.

Fairy tales teach us that we must always compromise ourselves for matters of the heart. Girls must first discover and then wallow in, their losses before we can be seen as gratuitously deserving of the riches of a "happily ever after". Take Cinderella for example, she not only had to lose a shoe in this month's, hottest fabrication - glass, but she also had to lose her dignity and then sanity when digesting the fact she had turned up to the Ball of the Century in a Pumpkin. She then lost any kudos points the slipper had gained her, by having to rush out pre-midnight. Curfews are *not* cool.
But don't fret! Cinderella did not lose the more intellectual parts of herself in vain, for at the end of this darkness came the gallantly anticipated light - a relatively handsome but more importantly, wealthy Prince. Mhmm, nothing illuminates an empty, chore ridden life quite like Royal dick. All is well in the world now that Cinderella has married rich. She no longer has to spend all morning and afternoon on her knees scrubbing floors for the wicked Step-Family. Oh no,

"Princess" Cinders now has the envious joy of switching once laboriously drenched tasks, for the thrilling new endeavour of spending all morning and afternoon scrubbing floors, *but*, all evening, on her knees doing something quite different indeed. Yay for progress!

It is sad that these lessons are so unsolicitedly scripted upon us before we are even wise, experienced, or brave enough to pen our own love stories. Cinderella teaches us that only love can save us from our shit lives and at no bank breaking cost, other than compromise. I mean Cinderella did not even know this man! She had heard he was a Prince a Charming one at that, and that was enough for her to encourage such witchcraftery of turning house mice into stallions. The thought of being able to move *out* of her current situation and *up* the social status ladder was enough for her to sneak out of the house and risk child-line informing beats, from her parents' drum.

But none of this fucked up bout of unfilliable insecurity is actually Prince Charming's fault. I mean don't get me wrong, hosting a million pound mansion party with the hopes of marrying the prettiest girl in the room has it's narcissistic, self orbitising issues, but let me be clear, Cinderella ain't shit either.
She sees Prince Charming as her way out, her sanctuary, her redeemer. She calls upon the moonlighting fairies and weeps for a modestly beat face and flatteringly, (we see that in-built corset Girl) tile sweeping dress. She puts her best face and foot forward in a façade so unfathomably laughable, who would think it would actually work. Cinderella teaches us that all we need to secure our very own "happily ever after" is a

pretty face, pretty dress and pretty good product mis-placement.

Is it Cinderella's fault that these "morals" have now been instilled in young women across the globe? Well to be frank - yes, but she's not the only one.
Fairy tales may have been the beginning of the mythical implementation of women only being as worthy as they look, but with the advances of web 2.0, we now have this message thrown at us from a multitude of angles.

Take a more recent love story, say, Stephenie Meyer's cult hit, Twilight for example.
In this new wave romatical fiction book, the main character, the Prince Charming of this saga, Edward Cullen develops a blood boiling obsession with the lead, Bella Swan. Bella is described as insanely "beautiful". We are lead to believe her beauty stops oncoming traffic and vampires dead in their tracks. Unfortunately, this was not reciprocated in the blockbuster movies and fans of the books were unfairly forced to endure a lip biting Kristen Stewart for the entire five films.
Bella uses her seemingly powerful "beauty" to capture the heart of her very own beast. However, whilst Edward struggles to literally not suck the life out of her, Bella acquires another fan of her beauty, Jacob. Except Jacob doesn't just want Bella for the overpowering scent of her hemogolobin, or her ever so strikingly symmetrical face, he wants her (for reasons unknown to me) for her rather dull personality. Jacob likes Bella for Bella. Clearly there is no dilemma! I mean let's put aside the fact she is essentially choosing between a 500 year old blood sucking peadophile and a tongue wagging

werewolf and assess the real facts here. Edward spends the whole story being suffocatingly defensive of Bella, there is *that* scene in the car park and countless other times where he just won't let her be, or breathe for fear of losing her, whereas Jacob wants nothing more than to love Bella unconditionally, exactly as she is.

Edward lives in a gated community at the top of a mountain. He has a grand piano in his room and drives some kind of shiny expensive car. Jacob is a poor village boy who spends his summers fixing up old motorcycles - not hunting in the Hamptons. Edward is cold. Jacob is hot.
Bella chooses Edward. Guess the bitch loves frostbite.

Fiction and fables may be the tools that are instructing us to be crazy, sexy and uncool in love but it is undebatable that the prowess of Hollywood Scripture is what teaches us how to love, dangerously.
We are taught how to be relentless, resilient sidekicks unworthy of taking the leather coated wheel and appreciating of the demises of leaning back in the passenger seat.
We have the unwarranted images of scantily dressed supporting actresses, caressing the big, burden bearing shoulders of the main act shoved down our throats at any given instance.
This main act, the leading man is often criminally flawed. Let's take the majority of Jason Statham characters for example. Always the violent, hot tempered Mr Wrong who is able to mask his imperfections by posing as Mr Right Now, for any tousled haired idiot of a woman willing to risk her soul for some rough, tumble and vanilla. At some point in the film, the object of Statham's desire is usually kidnapped and

his only way of apologising for putting her life at risk is to love her, hard and deep.

The learning objective here? Danger is an inevitable route to passion. The notion gathered from these films is that the only way to have, exhilarating, "Papi Screaming", orgasms is to almost have your head blown off by the Brazilian Mafia.

We all know the girls who choose the wrong men. The girls who mistake their irreparable need to be loved for their misconceived feelings of lust. Girls who believe that a rich or dangerous man is the only person who can save them. It's time to write new stories, new movies, hell, new reality tv series, it's time to re-write the female love encounter and teach girls that we do not only have to be vulnerable in love. That we can be strong, independent and powerful in love too.

Cinderella is entitled to her Prince Charming but maybe it's time for a new beginning and middle to her, "happily ever after" ending. How would it feel to grow up with the tales of an imperiously amiable Princess, with her own career and *own* blueprint to her escape from her shit life? She can fall in love, but at no compromise to her integrity or education. She will fall, drown and suffocate with consent in her adoration for her Prince but all the while she is aware that, *he* acquired her title and not the other way round.

Women have come so far in so many areas. We have been able to re-write a plague of oppressed histories but the plight is by no means over. We have made so many positive revolutions, so many political movements but still in *love* we are encouraged to play dumb. I say this as delicately as possible, but it's time to grab your pitch forks and scream

17

"Fuck Walt Disney" from your Barbie pink megaphones. The thought of doing so may set your childhood memories in flames, but think of how many you will save.

 Race

I remember the first time I was made aware that my skin colour could be a problem. I was a regular 10 year old girl, full of as much pre-teened excitement and naivety as the next stage school induced kid.

One day, whilst running around the playground with my bestest friend, she decided it would be a good idea to "find me a boyfriend". Now if I'm honest with you, I wasn't too charmed by the idea. I had just broken up with my imaginary boyfriend, (he found out I kissed his twin under the monkey bars) and I was taking some time out to focus on me. Nonetheless, I encouraged my friend's infantile tomfoolery and begun to enthusiastically, search the school quarters for an appropriate suitor.

When my friend laid eyes on this particular hunk of an adolescent boy, she decided he would be the one as he wasn't too consumed with the lunch time intensity of a patball or bull dog tournament. Even at that age, convenience trumped compatibility. As she started conversation with the lad, I tried my best to exude Frenchish cool. I took off my spectacles, wiped them on my jumper and tried to look as disinterested as possible, even though, by this stage my palms were drenched with the anticipation of an actual, real life boyfriend. Finally I thought, someone to jump up and down with at the school disco! My mind had already wandered to what I would wear... I was going through a blindly dedicated tomboy phase, so I was likely to debut my Manchester United shirt for our first dance. I then started to panic about what he would have thought of this. Did he also scribble MUFC on the inner sleeve of his maths book? Conflicts of interest so early into our relationship would cause such a gratuitous strain and could lead to early separation. I could probably forgive him if he supported Liverpool FC though; Jamie Redknapp is pretty damn hot...

So there I was all daydreamed and away with the potential wardrobe fairies when suddenly, my soap sudded bubble was popped by a rather barbaric prick.

"...Because she's black. I don't have black girlfriends".

Now I had awoken from my reverie, I had a chance to look at this boy in full focus. With the amount of dried bogey, habituating on the roof of his nostrils, I was pretty sure he didn't have *any* girlfriends, but nevertheless, his crass statement still knocked me for six.

"I'm not black! I'm brown!" I screamed.
I was equal parts mortified and dismayed. I pointed to my polished black footwear and defiantly showed him the difference between my shoe hue and skin shade. How could he call me black?! What an ignorantly oblivious juvenile! How can my sun-kissed glow be related to the colour of coal?
I had worked myself into a sort of violent, exasperated state. However, my expedient protest was received by big, blue, blank stares and a shrug of the shoulders.

I could never imagine that my God given melanin could be the cause of such cold blooded, treacherous exclusion. Thankfully, "I don't have black girlfriends" is not the general consensus for civilised men across the land but I can't help but wonder how much has *really* changed since then.

In my opinion, direct racism is less of a problem for Generation Y. We have grown to fuse our differences into one and we have successfully created a culture where colour of skin has become far less significant than eyebrow arches and acrylic nail shapes. We have the undying pleasure of growing up and into a culture where nobody cares what shade of brown, pink or yellow you are as long as you are pretty, rich and well-travelled. Any conflict that we suffer in accordance to our race rarely comes from our peers. In fact, almost all of the racial issues I have felt in my lifetime have been in the work place.

I have exhausted myself out of many jobs because I no longer had the energy to keep up my multiple personality charade. I have grown tired of pretending to be consistently well spoken, well-mannered and well groomed. There are times when the urge to flick my hair, drop some colloquial lingo and bring in rice and stew in a plastic container, far outweighs my desire to move up the career ladder. The constant feeling of judgement for something out of my control is immensely exhausting but for years, I continued to play the game, with hopes of scoring an extra point. After a while, I realised there is no winning a game that you do not know the rules to. Come into work on a Monday morning and "act too black" and have your fellow co-workers looking at you like something half eaten the cat has dragged in, come in on a

Tuesday and "act too white" and those same colleagues will whisper words of advice that you need to "be yourself". After all, if you're not going to act as black as you are, things could get pretty awkward when they need that token of support to sing along when N*ggas in Paris comes on the office radio.

The problem with all this is not that I have an issue being myself around other races, or even that other races have an issue with me being myself, it simply falls to the fact that I feel an insane amount of pressure to represent every single black girl with every single one of my actions. Snap my fingers, shut down and clap back too often and I am immediately a "typical" black girl and this must be how "we" all are, rude and angry.

I used to worry about how I am perceived to other races until I realised that what people think of me and my mannerisms does not actually design who I have created and built myself to be. Black people do not only come in different shades and sizes but also different ways of speaking, acting and behaving. Just like White or Asian communities, we have lawyers, doctors and serial killers. One rude black girl in the queue at McDonald's does not speak for an entire race, just like one white school shooter or Muslim terrorist doesn't speak for theirs.
Stereotypes are never as accurate as we would believe and I do think that GenY are one of the few social groups who have grasped this notion enthusiastically. Unfortunately it seems as though the media is still trailing far, far behind.

What often happens, specifically in western hemisphere

media is that in a bid to include the "Black Race", the industry veritably *excludes* us.

In television programs, we are typically represented by, falsely stereotypical caricatures who actually reflect the smallest minority of the minority, as if attaining a certain skin colour is a full time occupation that limits us to only moonlighting as gangsters, single parents, musicians or athletes.

Take popular British soap Eastenders for example. Considering the television sitcom is based in London, one of the most cosmopolitan cities on this planet, this is not well illustrated in the good old borough of make-believe Walford. If life were to be judged on TV shows being an accurate depiction of real life, then one might think that only two ethnic minority families can co-exist at any one time. One black (West Indian or African, never the two, never a combination) and one Asian. Whenever there is an accidental overflow of one or the other, a hurried storyline involving black cabs, gangs or fires, usually arises to re-adjust the quota.

One character, who failed to escape his inevitable fate, is Dexter Hartman, played by young, talented actor/comedian, Khali Best. Now although his timely departure greatly disconcerts me, having him in the show was far more detrimental to my sanity, anger and embarrassment levels.

Dexter Hartman was the single most, soul destroying character that had ever had the unfortunate task of pounding the E20 pavement. Hartman was frequently kissing his teeth, screwing up his face and using such failed colloquial terminology that many people I know, innocuously threatened to "show him how we really speak in the hood". If you haven't watched the show, don't, but I can assure you that it was that bad. I mean just because one is forming speech with words such as "blud", "fam" and "outchea", doesn't mean basic grammar and "street etiquette" should be abstained.

In a bid to include a youthful, black character, the chief writers of Eastenders, had managed to exclude any black person who knows how to form compound sentences and hold a conversation without wriggling one's neck.

But the buck doesn't stop with silver screen characters. On the big screen, the role of the negro seems to be limited to just three criterion: field slave, house slave and free slave (of course not counting the bad cops, gangsters, screw up sportsmen and "waiting to be raped Tyler Perry women). I don't know what it is about Hollywood, but it seems that the only way a group of black people can truly be acknowledged for their acting talents is when recreating cotton picking memories.

In her reputable book, Bad Feminist, Roxane Gay best sums this up as black people following Hollywood's rules, by starring in films that make slavery seem ay-okay because a magical white man or woman, managed to muster up some community absent decency and rescue a slave from a few more leather lashings.

The whole ceremony of watching these ironically white washed films and struggling to genuinely imitate the wails and and gasps from Caucasians in the theatre is immensely tiring. That being said, I am desperate for films that highlight my race in a multitude of shining lights. We are not *just* slaves.

As Chimamanda Ndechi said in her first TedTalk, it is very important to tell more stories of Africa. She passionately spoke of the fact that literature is about humanity and not just race. Africans fall in love, we move home, we find new jobs and *we too* experience a wealth of engaging emotions worthy of being noted in novels, television shows and blockbuster films. We are not just poor and hungry. We are humans.

Sadly, the racial bias also stretches into printed publications. On the online version of continuously controversial, Vogue Italia, editor Franca Sozzani, has created "Vogue Black", an area of the site designed "exclusively for black people", featuring content, images and polls specifically for the "black experience". So again, in a bid to include the entire, "coloured" species, Sozzani has managed to exclude the majority of it.

As shocking as it sounds, many of us don't actually want to know the "best hairstyles for relaxed hair" or how to "dress for our curves" and by segregating topics, models and news stories that appear to be more relevant to "us", Condènast unknowingly fans the flames of inequality.

 Other than the media, there is one more outlet that permanently expels the black race -Feminism.
When I speak to (at) my black friends about Strident Feminism, many of them groan heartily whilst synonymously closing their ears and drifting off. So many of my peers feel as though the ideals of Feminism do not speak to (but rather, at) them and do not consider the unique cultural needs of a woman of colour. For example, many gender biases that *we* are taught growing up, become rooted in tradition. Women need to be able to maintain the household and bear children

regardless of their desire to reach the top of the career ladder. A large portion of us can take this ideal a little too unerringly and see this ancestral requirement as a cultural duty. Of course, a lot of us *do* know that Feminism was initially designed to give women the *choice* to do as they please based on self inclination, rather than obligatory genitalia function but through years of radicalisation and patriarchy press slander, this message has gotten lost in translation. Also, many of the popular, most notable "celebrity" Feminists are white, middle class women. As we all know, it can be extremely difficult to truly hear the sub text of a revolution if one does not feel that the speaker is able to relate to the listener.

Feminism needs to realise that women are not just women just like black people are not just black. We are housewives, career giants, heterosexuals, lesbians, white *and* coloured. We are more than our oppression, we are more than what we spend 8-12 hours a day doing, we are more than our skin colours.

If even the grown-ups of TV, film, print and "equalist" groups cannot grasp the concept of fair representation and actual, *inclusive* inclusion, then how can we ever expect to move on from a stage where little shits of the playground turn down imaginative young girls, based on the colour of their skin, rather than the content of their character?

Beauty's Interlude

"It's not my responsibility to be beautiful. I'm not alive for that purpose. My existence is not about how desirable you find me."
- Warsan Shire

Beauty is a funny old thing isn't it? For something that is completely beyond our control, the quest for it can quickly take over our lives. I have heard beauty referred to as a talent, a skill, a gene and a pot of gold at the end of the rainbow. Beauty is the gift that keeps on giving. A present for your presence, used as a surface level veil to mask the decaying personalities of women.

Beauty is no longer unique to the individual. Beauty is no longer in the eye of the beholder but now belongs to the 40,000 social media followers who await a bad eyebrow sketch or lopsided boob to de-throne one from their once perfect appeal. Beauty has taken over our thoughts and actions in a way that feels new to me, but is just an old trick being regurgitated by society. The beauty trap is here to stay my friends, but it is far more soul destroying to know that it never quite left.

Discussing beauty is a cripplingly awkward subject for me and I have no doubt that addressing this beast head and mind on, will open up a can of worms that I do not have enough will or insect repellent to deal with.
I wish I could call myself beautiful and base this chapter on what this word means to me and my life but I cannot. Somewhere along the way I did not get the memo to be confident in my appearance. Instead, I was encouraged to downplay any aesthetic charm I have and promote the parts of my personality that can equally be seen as gifts. I can call myself funny with much ease and little grace, I have no issue displaying my intellect or wit and I have never stuttered when having to highlight my academic of professional achievements. I big myself up on job applications without a flicker of doubt and embellishing my skills comes as an absolute second nature to me, but for some unexplained, inbuilt reason, I have real trouble discussing or accepting my beauty.

I subconsciously reject compliments on my exterior because I have no desire to be known or seen as my face or body. I have never wanted people to look at me and see pretty. I want you to see passion. But surely one does not need to compromise the other, particularly in an age where women are being both forced and denied the right of "having it all"?

I do not stop traffic and my milkshake brings no boys to the yard. And you know what, neither of these statements bothers me, I mean, the less often I have to clean my nutribullet the better! Time spent plucking and preening can be better expelled through the arts of the soul.
Creative writing is my superpower and I do not need the new Bobby Brown 187 angled eyeshadow brush to prove it.

Youth

I don't want to sit here, 40 years from now, watching carry on films with hysterical tears rolling down my face as I compare Barbara Windsor's in-humanely perky tits to my own below the knee mamory glands.

I don't want to look back at my youth and feel the deepest, darkest of regrets as to why I didn't start Botox and laughter line fillers at 19 like the rest of my peers. I don't want to be a pensive pensioner who spends more time fretting over the magical silver in my fluffy coif than the fact that my grandchild is seven and cannot sit still without the iPad xGen 3000 with quadruple retina Hdxi screen.

I want to grow old gracefully, whilst growing into myself and exhaling an expressional amount of self-love and empowerment.

For me, it is very important to become the type of woman I wish I knew in my teens. However, the reasons I have never met this woman vary. First of all, I believe I was and am looking for her in the wrong places. Every week we read stories in the news about a new rogue celebrity who is growing up in the public eye and living out their peaks and troughs under the microscope of judgement. Take Miley Cyrus for instance; she is constantly abused by "Internet Mothers" who bash her and her legend of a father, for not heeding to her involuntary title of role model. Miley Cyrus is constantly clad in designer leotards, with nipples, underarm hair and hip flexors being thrust into our conscience. She is a young girl trying to scope out her place in the world with enough money in her Hannah Montana savings fund for her to experiment with a new identity more often than she changes music genre. She is a performer, a musician, an artist, why would that make her an automatic holder of the youth future?

Miley, being a firm embracer and enabler of the spotlight quite obviously has a major influence on her generation. I mean, even I went through a stage of complete and utter obsession with the teen star. I used to brag to colleagues about how many times a week I had to search her on google images to ensure I hadn't missed any changes to her hair or clothing style. Miley fascinated me on a level that I could neither understand nor justify. There was something about her that left me feeling slightly intoxicated and as I drank up her image, sometimes three or four times a day, I began to believe I could replicate and reflect whatever it was about her that I loved.

To be drunk on a celebrity is a psychologically wonderful and insightful thing.
See, my love for Miley stems from a burning, love, no desirous, determination… acrobatic ambition to be the type of woman that gives not a single beaver busting damn about the opinion, judgement or scrutinisation of another human being. These are the celebrities I am drawn to. The free spirits, the rebels, the women who look society in the eye and expend their entire God given energy to bending and breaking the rules. I don't engross myself in depictions of

Miley, Rihanna, Amandla Stenberg and Zoe Kravitz because of their undyingly mystical beauty, I find myself unpacifyingly obsessed with these young women because they successfully portray a level of air and disgrace that I only dream of achieving. They have become my accidental, depthless role models because they unintentionally represent the very aesthetic I want to convey in my own art.

I write as a form of solace but I also write as an extension of my personality. I may be far too wimpy to pick up a blunt or let my armpit hair grow out, but I can adapt that kind of careless, fearless courage to my own performance. I bash the keyboard violently and release the thoughts, once restrained by the cuffs of social humanity. With each word I type, I break the chains of conformity. I embrace my anomalies. But these people are not role models, and neither do they want to be.

For those outside the gates of Generation Y, it is easy to blame social media and the influx of "do nothing bitches" who seem to be making power moves with the pace makers of the universe, for the seemingly innate sense of entitlement springing from the souls of my era. We live in a time where sex sells and sex tapes can transform you from "The Help" to "The CEO". And in a time where young people are more concerned with cheating the struggle and levelling up without the playing the game, why wouldn't that look like a beneficial route to explore?

My generation is deemed lazy, narcissistic, disrespectful and undeserving. The New York Times referred to us as "Generation Why Bother" and the New York Post labelled us "the worst generation". We are the children who were

32

brought up in stage schools, poetry clubs and sports centres. We are the sons and daughters who were pushed to attend after school reading, acting and swimming clubs by pushy parents who share desks at work. It was instilled in us that the sky cannot be the limit since there are footprints on the moon. Pushed to aim high, creatively and academically, we were told that the averages of life were not good enough for us, we needed to dream big and bold to be able to survive. And so we did.

My generation went to University with nothing more than a shallow knowledge of supply, demand and Shakespeare. We transformed our a-level results into specialisations in drama, accounting and biomedical physics. We kept our heads in the books, our feet in the club and our hands on our part time jobs. We are the generation who sit in group discussions in the library until 2am and go back to our shared accommodation rooms and work on our ambitions of rapping, scoring or writing. Some of us sacrificed our dreams for degrees; some of us left the campus life, to carve a different route to educational knowledge. We juggled it all because we were told we could have it. We are rioters and activists. We choose our causes with more care than boyfriends or selfies. We have heart. We have passion. Lazy? Bish where?

My generation is hell bent on doing what we love for a living. We want to fall into careers and lifestyles based on love and passion and refuse to settle for less, despite those same pushy, desk sharing parents, insisting it's time for us to get a "proper job". We would rather rest on our laurels, sketching and scheming business plans, than sit in an office with two screens and a phone. We want more.

And how do the adults who nurtured us in this way feel about it? Well, they hate us, probably even resent us because we are chasing awards, trophies, medals and plaques with way more bravado, braggadocio and bluntly put, balls than they ever could. In a time where we are unable to own anything due to fucked up interest rates and credit scores, we take on the world fearlessly knowing that having nothing can only mean having nothing to lose.

In an article titled "Solving Gen Y's Passion Problem", in the Harvard Business Review, Cal Newport discusses the fact that the term "follow your passion" was published more during the late 90s and early 2000s than in any other period, just when Gen Y was conquering early school years.
We have always been told to prioritise the passion and spend our time focusing on finding that, rather than work. Newport calls this a bout of misinformation. He urges us to take this as a starting point to create new conversations about careers, he says we don't need slogans we need facts.

I of course, do not agree. I see nothing wrong with the phrase or slogan and think it can only be foolish to blame words for the plight Gen Y are marching through. We may stay at home, unemployed and unbothered, scrolling through social media, liking, favouriting and re-tweeting unattainable images of six packs and six figure homes but at least we have something to aim for other than 2.4 children and a council flat in the east end.

I loved Miley because she taught me how to grow

unapologetically and ruthlessly. It doesn't matter if you were a teen Disney star then, a gyrating, tongue wagging "little madam" now or a book loving, mixtape writing unsociable adult tomorrow. All that matters is that you are constantly evolving at a pace you find comfortable. We are supposed to change and we are supposed to dream. Take your lessons in life from whoever is giving them out. If you are learning how to pay off your mother's mortgage from Kim Kardashian, or discovering how to use your manufactured good looks and semi sassy personality to open up an online clothing boutique from this year's, Instagram "It Girl", then so be it. Passion is not the problem and neither is the source of inspiration. We can all upgrade our minds, bodies and lifestyles if we are willing to carve out our own destinies.

Equip yourself with the right tools and turn your passion into a profession. And if watching YouTube videos on "The perfect eyebrow arch" is what helps you get there, then keep doing that.

Men

I don't know how the men of this world are supposed to be but I know how I write them.

For instance, if this year had been a chapter from my book of adoring prose, my life partner, would not have spent every particle of his time, looking for flights to Miami FL, whilst annoyingly *and* disrespectfully misquoting the Bae - Drake - Trophies. No no, I can blissfully assure you that a man of my word, would not be making any plans to go to "Dreams with a suitcase" filled with crumpled one dollar bills.
Instead, my penned fairy-tale would entail a knight in rose gold armour, hopping in his car or chariot - whatever - being careful to not be wearing a single item of offensive clothing, stopping by Cinders' local Chinese place and pulling up to her royal palace with said takeaway treats and an award winning bouquet, carefully arranged to spell out some loving message. Impractical yes, but the thoughtfulness is hot, too hot. He would then throw her table top ornaments to the ground and hoist her up onto it. Mr Right here and Right now would then proceed to Plough my fictional Cinderella to Abu Dhabi.

My mind involuntarily invents several stories like this. My favourite is the one where, after Prince Charming and Cinderella's seasoned fall-out, instead of activating his

predictable immovable stubbornness, PC - for once, allows
Cinderella to take the centre stage of Nonsensical Adamancy.
Then he would of course reward her with a bouquet of
diamond roses before heavily serenading his queen with a
vintage ukulele that he retrieved from the davenport. Okay
that one *was* a little too fableised but you get the gist. In my
yet to be written dreams, a woman always gets her own way,
receives some kind of gift and then gets elevated onto a
furnishing of her fancy to be fucked - hard.

Lucky for me, or my partner rather, I have many friends who
audaciously explain to me (at least twice a week) that I cannot
live in the sauce - another Simpsons' reference for you.
The thing is, I don't actually *want* to change my beaux. He's
beautiful - a slimmly cut Adonis who's hugs make me feel
safe... guarded. He's also funny - sometimes but not as often
as he thinks. And most importantly, He's insanely and
"blindly in lovingly" tolerant.

You see, to love a writer is not the easiest of tasks and to feel
uncomfortably inadequate because you're always being
compared to Fitzwilliam Darcy is even less manageable. But
he *does* manage.
Somehow, in his own enchanting way, he *manages* to see past
the Writers' cock-blocking Insanity and believe you me, that
is a story worth way more than jewel encrusted roses and
won ton soup.

I'm sure I am not the only woman to habituate in the reverie.
We need to cut men some serious slack but I know that
although I see the problem. I am also a part of it. As
someone who stands up on anything that can hold my weight

to shout about my love for women and the need for a resurrected sisterhood, I can sometimes be seen as someone who does not care about the lifting up and empowerment of men. I have often been told that men go through a very hard time too and in order for a true change to happen, they also need feminist support.

And they're right.

For too long, too many Feminist Extremists have blamed men for all that is wrong with the world. When feminism should solely concern the equality of sexes, through the act of a handful of angry, bitter women, we have actually spent more time attempting to inferioralise the male species. We blame the entire gender for things caused by a minority. We scream that chivalry is dead, that men are dirty perverse rapists and no good fathers. We base our judgements of men in the present on those from our past. We alienate a future of togetherness, we disregard the true meaning of feminism.

Women have been oppressed for centuries and it is truly beautiful to notice any type of change but we must realise that the aim of the game is to lift ourselves up to a level equal to not greater than men.

How would you feel if your son grew up to be battled and banished by women for the mere fact of the bulge in his boxers?

Women are lucky because we have each other. We have networks and non blood "sisters" and mentors and friends who will grab us by the scruff of the neck as soon as we start to slip. Those who will hug us and tell us it's okay. Twitter accounts who will anonymously give us advice and motivational words when we are feeling particularly down and most of all we have chocolate, no matter how crummy, bummy or lonely we are feeling, we always have chocolate coated reassurance.

But what or who do the men have? Men are known for not sharing their inner most delicate feelings. The pressures of being perceived as, as masculine as those gym built muscles are, is suffocating. Men have been told that they cannot cry or express any feeling other than anger. If anything, the gender limitations towards men are far more rigid and socially disapproving than that for women. In 2016 women are blessed to live in a world where we can wake up and decide to have any career without so much of a bat of a mink eyelash. We are policemen, firemen and businessmen. But how many men feel comfortable about working in stereotypically female work industries? How many male nannies, secretaries or midwives do you know?

In the same breath that I use to push out the passionate beliefs that women can be and do whatever we wish and that what we involuntarily pack in our panties cannot limit us to a life of housewifery or motherhood, I scream that this should be the same for men also. Men should be able to be romantic or sentimental without uncalled for judgement from friends, just like they should be able to be introverted and non gentlemen like, without stick from the ladies. Feminism and the fundamentals of equality cannot truly progress, develop or become a true, accepted ideal until the notion of gender stereotypes are completely dropped. I write my man any way I want depending on my mood. He is more than the last argument we had or the beautiful bouquet he delivered, not just on paper but in real life too. He is more than my judgements, more than my daddy issues and more than my past.

I love men. I love women. And a true, people empowering feminist could never say any different.

Women

Every now and then, I stumble across something on social media that makes me first stare blankly, wondering if the megapixels on my 6inch screen have perplexed my brain cell activity so ferociously that I may go blind, and then throw up with a motivation that can only be referred to as impure frustration. It sounds exceedingly dramatic but I can assure you all hyperbolic feelings can be justified. I mean, just when I was starting to think that the world is moving forward and actually taking this influx of twenty-something, rowdy, nipple freeing, feminists seriously, one colossal idiot is attempting to single handily, send us flying back forty paces, no gun salute.

Amber Rose may sound like this season's hottest colour blocking trend but believe me, there is nothing "in" about this attention seeking, has been.

When Amber Rose first started her unsolicited, force fed attack of her warped version of female empowerment, I was actually behind her. Knowing the history and origin of the "Slut Walk" campaigns, first started in 2011, Toronto, Ontario, after a police officer told a woman that "women should stop dressing like sluts" to avoid being sexually assaulted and raped, it was hard not to support an essential movement which has already been franchised globally.

However, judging by Ms Rose's Instagram page, many spectators were unaware of the ancestry of the rally and immediately called "Muva Rosebud" out, for, well, being a slut. But like I said, because I knew that the efforts of her own Slut Walk come from a good, well-meaning place, I chose not to chime in on the back-chatter. In fact, I pretty much remained indifferent to Amber Rose, her actions, and baby papa drama, until she uncouthly, rattled my cage by announcing she will be releasing a book entitled, "How to be a Bad Bitch".

"How to be a Bad Bitch", which is available on Amazon now for those who do not wish to respect their intellect or genitalia, promises to deliver "expert advice on finances, career, love, beauty and fashion". The could be rags to riches story, the blurb cites her "South Philly" routes, has been dubbed the "edgy yet accessible bad bitch guide to life, love and success". Life, love and success according to Amber Rose? Is this the urban community's answer to Sheryl Sandberg's Lean In? A book that will inspire and ignite a sense of go hard, entrepreneurship in young women across the globe? You may think I'm being sarcastic, but the funnily dangerous thing about this book is that people will be inspired and something will ignite in our young people.

Amber Rose has made a career out of being somebody's wife and or girlfriend. She nakedly paraded into our forgivingly fickle spotlight as Kanye West's significant other back in 2008, and has spent the last five years hopping between, rappers, thongs and thirst traps. Prior to her two year relationship with Yeezus, Amber Rose spent her nights sliding up and down poles at various different strip clubs, where I assume a plethora of "bad bitches" are born. Is this really the route to success?

Now, I'm never one to knock another's hustle, I understand that we all have bills to pay and when it's all said and done, all we are trying to do is "eat" but honestly, there are better meal options. My irritation stems less from Muva as a person and a lot more from the message she is bellowing out to young, impressionable females.

As someone who tries to empower females at any given opportunity, I can tell you that it is not always easy. Being a feminist doesn't make me perfect and I am definitely filled to the brim with contradictions but my goodness, sometimes I find myself looking down from my sky high stallion and wanting to scream "can't we all just get along —normally?!".

With this aggressive rise of the wannabe bad bitches, I am finding that fewer and fewer women have any desire to make new friends with their fellow gender. You see, what I've gathered from the internet is that being a bad bitch, has a lot to do with doing anything in your power to get ahead, more often that not, this involves stepping on someone to get up. Women are becoming more ruthless and not a day goes by without me seeing some unattractively fonted quote about "getting what I want" or "taking what I want" blasted all over that same 6inch screen.

My message is simple and involves limited to zero amounts of self slut admission. There is enough space for all of us to reach the towering heights of our wildest dreams and the way

to climb up is not to step on, but to stretch out an
accessorised arm and lift another bitch up!

Outro

I cannot explain my motives behind self-publishing this mini book, beyond reasons other than wanting to showcase something I have created. My frustration when trying to plot the best way to release my art to the world almost killed me, but the sheer motivation of wanting to have something that I produced, kept me going.

Budding artists host exhibitions and showcase new sketches on Instagram. Upcoming musicians spend days in home built studios, and nights uploading semi-mixed tracks onto Soundcloud. Wannabe actors and television personalities take their over-enthusiastic staged smiles and stories to YouTube. But where can a writer find such elevated exposure? Wordpress? Believe me, it's not the same.

I have always struggled to maintain a blog because I felt a complete disconnect with the artistry of writing. Blogging is a business, and I always find myself more concerned with views, likes and reposts, rather than the subject at hand. I alter the way I paint, in a bid to achieve public recognition for my brush strokes. Blogging also feels like a chore which in turn withdraws all the technical craft from word play. I like to free write in retaliation to the burdens of my bumble busy mind or bubble beneath my agitated skin.

I have always enjoyed and appreciated the power of words and never quite understood the old "sticks and stones" phrase. Words can indeed hurt, especially if that is what they were intended to do. Words can also conceive a wealth of various emotions. Words can start wars and fires, but with a different tone, intent and enunciation, words can calm nations and unite enemies.

I write with the intention to be felt.

Thank you for reading x

Personal Notes

Personal Notes

Printed in Great Britain
by Amazon